Other titles by the authors published by
Nova Foresta Publishing unless otherwise stated.

Georgina Babey
Churches of the New Forest (writing as G Peckham)
A New Forest Christmas (Halsgrove Publishing)
Ashurst and Colbury: A Celebration of the Last 100 Years
Images of England: New Forest (Tempus Publishing)

Peter Roberts
Ashurst: A New Forest Railway Village 1789-1939
Minstead: Life in a 17th Century New Forest Community

LYNDHURST

A Brief History and Guide

by

Georgina Babey & Peter Roberts

Nova Foresta Publishing

First published 2003 by
Nova Foresta Publishing
185 Lyndhurst Road, Ashurst, Southampton, SO40 7AR
www.novaforestabooks.co.uk

Printed by Sarum Colourview

ISBN 0 9523173 5 4

Designed and typeset by the authors
All contemporary photographs were taken by the authors
Front cover: Bolton's Bench
Back cover: Lyndhurst High Street

Contents

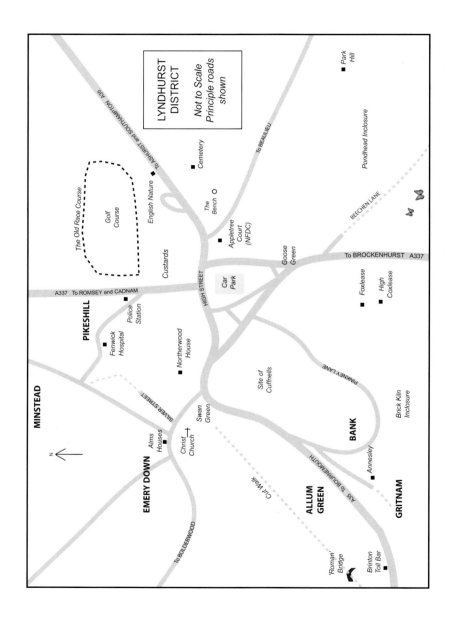

Acknowledgements

We would like to record our gratitude to Roy Jackman for all the work he has carried out on the history of Lyndhurst during his long association with the recently disbanded Lyndhurst Historical Society, and for his enthusiastic help with the research for this book. We are also indebted to Anne Biffin, Pam Bloomfield, David Dickenson, Anne Dickson, Alan Foot, Dick Galton, David Giles, Rosemary Manning, Robert Osborne, Mervyn Roberts, Jenni Tubbs, Cecil Whitfield and the Bursar of Coxlease School. Photographs on pages 12 and 13 are courtesy of the Verderers of the New Forest. Our thanks to any others we may have overlooked, we hope they will forgive us. Naturally any errors that remain are ours. Amendments and additions will be welcomed for possible inclusion in future editions.

Introduction and Brief History

"The people of Lyndhurst ought, I always think, to be the happiest and most contented in England"

So wrote John R Wise in his book *The New Forest: its History and Scenery* which was published in 1863. Wise was not a native of the New Forest but had fallen under its spell from his very first visit. He often came to Lyndhurst, sometimes staying at the South View Guest House in Gosport Lane, which he used as his base to explore the surrounding woods and heaths.

Like John Wise countless visitors have fallen under the spell of the New Forest and, for many, their experience begins in Lyndhurst, the administrative 'capital'. A first glance at the High Street might lead one to suspect that its origins lay in the Victorian era but closer inspection reveals many 17th and 18th century buildings. The oldest building is the ancient Court of Verderers attached to the Queen's House at the west end of the High Street and near to the parish church of St Michael and All Angels.

The name Lyndhurst, probably of Saxon origin, means 'lime-wood'. Although, nowadays, large stands or woods of lime are absent from Britain's pasture woods, individual examples of the native small-leaved lime (*Tilia cordata*) can be found around the village. Indicators of early settlement around Lyndhurst are in evidence. On Matley Heath, between Lyndhurst and Beaulieu, the mounds of Bronze Age round barrows can be seen and at Pondhead, near Matley, Roman coins have been excavated.

In 980, the recorded history of Lyndhurst begins. It was, by this time, a royal manor granted to the Abbey of Amesbury in Wiltshire. In 1079 the first Norman king, William I, designated the whole area between the river Avon on the west, Wiltshire to the north, and to the south and east the Test, Southampton Water and the Solent as his "New" Forest, or Nova Foresta, to serve as a safe dwelling place for the beasts of the chase.

"Entering Lyndhurst... many of the picturesque associations of the past come to the mind and touch the fancy with pleasant suggestions. Through its winding, straggling street the Conqueror and the hunting members of his family must often have ridden..."

F G Heath's fanciful vision of Lyndhurst in *Autumnal Leaves***, 1881**

Lyndhurst High Street in the early 1900s. This postcard was produced by the printer E M Howard whose board appears so prominently on the right

Standing as it does at the meeting place of many major routes and tracks connecting Southampton, Beaulieu, Lymington, Christchurch, Ringwood, Fordingbridge, Salisbury, Romsey and Winchester, Lyndhurst's importance for administration purposes was quickly realised.

Over the centuries Lyndhurst became the haunt of royalty, nobility and commoner alike. It was also a magnet for artists, writers and professionals of all kinds. Most of the inhabitants of Lyndhurst were involved, unsurprisingly, in the timber and coppice industries. As the village increased in popularity there was an influx of newcomers who built large houses and consequently required domestic workers.

Many locals are still employed in the service industry providing accommodation, hospitality and goods for the many visitors.

The words of C J Phillips, taken from the 1876 edition of his *New Forest Handbook,* still hold true:

> *"I purposely advise visitors, whatever the time at their disposal, to make Lyndhurst the centre of their movements, by reason alike of its accessibility and of its proximity to some of the most charming scenes in the Forest."*

Alleyway by the Post Office in the High Street

3

A Walk in the High Street and Bolton's Bench

The Stag Hotel and Mailmans Arms

From the main car park take the vehicle exit. The New Forest Museum and Tourist Information office should be on your right. As you leave the car park you may wish to check the Parish Notice Board and town map for coming events and information. Turn right. On the opposite side of the street you will notice the diversity of roof heights, decorative ridge tiles and many other attractive architectural features. Right next door to the *Stag Hotel* is the *Mailmans Arms* - New Foresters are thirsty folk! Note the date plaque of 1907 on the front of the *Stag* - this was when major alterations took place, not the date of the original building.

Further down the High Street, past the Post Office is the *Court House Tea Rooms*. This building was once used as council offices, and also a news agency. Beyond *Forest Cottage B&B*, peeping through the trees, the roof and chimneys of *Holmfield* can be seen. Built in the

19th century, it was once the home of Sir Charles Burrard (whose family home was at Walhampton near Lymington) and his wife and six daughters. Later, Major George Meyrick, Master of the New Forest Foxhounds lived here. Subsequently it became a residential home, then a hotel and is now apartments.

You will now be standing outside the *Lyndhurst Park Hotel* on the A35 approach road. Again this building has undergone many changes from its beginnings as a large house called *Glasshayes*. In 1862 the house was owned by Mr Castleman. At this time a lane known as Love Lane ran behind the house. Mr Castleman, obviously rather a spoilsport, promised to give the church a new clock if they would close Love Lane "*in the interests of the morality of the village*". The church got its clock, which can still be seen on the church tower, and it is to be hoped that the lovers found an alternative venue. *Glasshayes* evolved (*c*1897) into a hotel at first called the *Grand Hotel*, later the *Lyndhurst Park*.

The Grand Hotel in the 1940s. It later became the Lyndhurst Park Hotel

Bolton's Bench, a steep mound topped by a clump of fenced yews and seats is across the Beaulieu Road. This is, possibly, Lyndhurst's most famous landmark. Wonderful views of the village and its surroundings can be obtained from the top. Appletree Court, now used as administrative offices of the NFDC, is tucked in the trees near the *Lyndhurst Park Hotel* and the stark, white walls of Northerwood House at Emery Down are clearly visible. Bolton's Bench commemorates one of the Duke's of Bolton who was Lord Warden of the New Forest and whose family were Master Keepers of Burley Bailiwick in the 18th century. The annexe to the cemetery, which is reached by walking past the memorial and up the hill, is the resting place of John Wise author of the standard work *The New Forest: its History and Scenery.* His grave is sited near the main entrance.

The Memorial and Bolton's Bench

Return to the High Street, crossing the road by the fire station. From this side of the road you will have a better view of the block of Victorian shops recently passed. Moving up the High Street note the particularly ornate facade of the building which now houses the Nat-West Bank, on the junction with Gosport Lane. As you pass the *Stag Hotel* again, you may notice a board attached to the outside of the side wall which gives a few details of the history of the pub.

6

Opposite is the Workman's Club which was established in 1890, and is housed in a rather elegant building. Next door is a much older building which currently houses Royal's bookshop and news agency. Budgens supermarket, once the site of the Plaza cinema and, before that, the New Forest Hall is on your right and the Austin & Wyatt estate agency is housed in the old *Volunteer Arms* public house. Lloyds Bank still bears, above the door, its old logo - the beehive. This symbol of industry dates back to 1765. By chance it appeared on the front of the Birmingham Gazette in which was announced on the front of the Birmingham Gazette in which was announced

the founding of Taylors and Lloyds Bank. It was believed to have been used for the first time by Lloyds Bank on its notes in 1822. Opposite is one of the oldest pubs in Lyndhurst the *Fox and Hounds*, once a staging inn.

Crossing the Romsey Road junction, the pavement narrows considerably and then mounts steps to the *Crown Hotel*. In front of the *Crown* there is a plaque carrying the date 1600. This is, possibly, when the *Crown* was first established, not the date of the current building which is late 19th century.

The beehive symbol above the door of Lloyds Bank

Note the mounting block outside the main entrance to the hotel where guests would alight from their carriages. A little further on, past the school, is Red Lodge, built by a Dr Maskew and used for a time as a home for inebriates. Later the Misses Burrard moved here from *Holmfield* when Sir Charles and Lady Burrard had both died.

The old mounting block outside the entrance to the Crown Hotel

The pedestrian crossing nearby will give a detour, if desired, to the church, Queen's House and the Verderers' Court. (For a history of these buildings, and the pubs and schools, see the appropriate chapters).

Opposite the Queen's House is *Elcombes* another of Lyndhurst's grand abodes now converted to apartments. Built in the 17th century it was home to a family of wealthy merchants, headed by John Elcombe. When John's grandson James, one time mayor of Romsey, died in the plague year 1665 he left, amongst other things, seven

Above, the splendid Georgian elegance of Elcombes, and right, the attractive Coach House doorway

feather beds, ten cows, two yoke of oxen, two pairs of wheels and a dung-pot - wealth indeed! The east wing was added around 1870 to accommodate the large domestic staff needed to service a high class Victorian establishment.

From the church retrace your steps to the car park using the High Street en-

The roof line visible from the High Street car park entrance

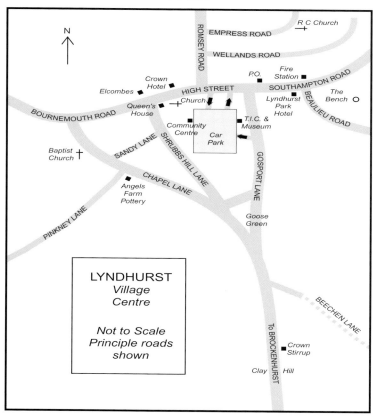

Chapter Two

The Queen's House and Verderers' Court

Queen's House

The building that gives Lyndhurst its unique historic interest is the Queen's House and the attached Verderers' Court. The Queen's House, at one time the monarch's Royal residence, is still owned by the Crown and now acts as the offices of the Deputy Surveyor and his Forestry Commission staff. Its name changes with the gender of the ruling monarch. The house was first documented in 1297 when an order was issued for *"twenty oaks to make laths for the use of the Queen's manor house at Lyndhurst."* At this time Edward I's queen, Eleanor of Castile, was staying at Lyndhurst while the king was away waging war. The manor house was probably superseded by a hunting lodge. Many state documents of the 14th century were written at Lyndhurst testifying to the frequency of the royal visits. In 1388 a hall was built adjacent to the house which later became known as the Verderers' Hall.

Queen's House, Verderers' Court and St Michael and All Angels

Although evidence of its medieval and Tudor structures remain, the house is now a remarkably complete example of 17th century architecture - in fact, the only surviving major building of the Charles I period to be seen anywhere in Hampshire.

Details on the rain heads at Queen's House reveal ownership by two previous Queens - Anne and Victoria - and indicate the dates of extension or repair

Verderers' Court

The Court of Verderers is one of the most ancient in the country and it still regularly meets to enforce modern Forest law and protect the Commoners' rights. The Common rights are those of Pasture, Mast, Estovers, and the now unused rights of Turbary and Marl. The right of Pasture allows the grazing of ponies, cattle, donkeys and in some cases, sheep on the Forest, the running of pigs during the pannage season to eat acorns and beech mast (Common of Mast), the taking of wood from the Forest for fuelwood (Estovers), the rights to cut turf for burning (Turbary), and the use of lime-rich clay for fertilisation (Marl).

Forest Law was introduced by the Norman kings for the purposes of providing special protection for the beasts of the forest, especially the royal deer, and also for the protection of their habitat - the woodland and heath, known as the vert. The word is from the French, meaning green, and the name of the Verderers has the same origin. The Verderer was a judicial officer, claiming parity with the office of Coroner, but while the Coroner was concerned with the administration of common law, the Verderer only dealt with matters under the specialised Laws of the Forest.

With the coming of the New Forest Act 1877, the Court of Verderers was entirely reconstituted. The Official Verderer was then appointed by the Crown and the other six Verderers elected by registered Commoners and the parliamentary voters of the parishes and townships wholly or partly within the Forest perambulation. The 1949 New Forest Act brought further changes to the Court to reflect the changing role of the Forest. Whereas, previously, the Forest was valued principally as a hunting preserve, and later for the production of timber, it was finally becoming recognised as an area of outstanding environmental importance.

The Verderers' Court in session in 1997
l-r, back row - Richard Stride, Peter Roberts, Dionis Macnair, John Burry (Official Verderer), Anthony Pasmore, David Stagg, Jeff Kitcher, John Perry
l-r, front row - Sue Westwood (Clerk), Arthur Barlow (Deputy Surveyor), Will Park (Land Agent)

The Court now consists of ten Verderers: the Official Verderer and four appointed members nominated by the Forestry Commission, Hampshire County Council, Countryside Agency and DEFRA. The other five Verderers are elected by the registered Commoners, and serve for a period of six years.

The Court is served by a full time Clerk with a part time assistant and, currently, five Agisters. The Agisters, who each ride their own designated area of Forest, are responsible for the welfare of depastured stock. They organise a series of drifts (round-ups) of stock each autumn throughout the Forest, tail marking and worming the animals, and removing them if their condition demands. Foals who are to remain on the Forest over winter are branded and tail marked. An annual charge, known as the marking fee, is made on each animal depastured and the money is used by the Verderers to employ the Agisters. Another, unenviable, responsibility of the Agisters is to attend the many road accidents involving Commoners stock.

'Rufus's' Stirrup which hangs on the wall of the Verderers' Hall

On the wall of the Verderers' Hall hangs a large antique iron stirrup. This is known as Rufus's Stirrup, although it is thought more likely to date from Tudor times, and it was used as a measure for dogs. The Forest law stood that no man was allowed to keep a dog of such a size as to be a nuisance to the king's deer, or likely to be used for illicit hunting. If the dog could pass through the stirrup it was deemed harmless. If it could not it was expeditated, *i.e.* its forefeet were maimed to prevent it being a successful hunter - an indication of the harshness of ancient Forest law - although, later, a fine was extracted as an alternative.

The first part of the modern court proceedings are open to the public and then, when the announcements have been made and the presentments heard,

The ancient steps which Commoners and others mount to make a presentment

the Verderers retire to deliberate. At present, the court meets on the third Wednesday of the month except in August, and the December court is not open to the public. It is also possible to look round the Court when it is not in session by contacting reception at the Queen's House for an appointment.

Each Court session is opened by the Head Agister who, with right arm raised, pronounces:

"Oyez, Oyez, Oyez,
All manner of persons who have any presentment to make,
or matter or thing to do at this Court of Verderers, let
them come forward and they shall be heard.
God Save the Queen."

Entrance to the Verderers' Court at the north end of Queen's House. Evidence of the hall's ancient origins can be seen in the brickwork to the right of the door

Chapter Three

The Churches

St Michael and All Angels

The parish church of Lyndhurst - dedicated to St Michael and All Angels - stands on an imposing height overlooking the village and opposite the *Crown Hotel* and the village school. There is evidence that a place of worship has been on the site from medieval times but the construction of the present building was begun in 1860 when it replaced a smaller, grey stone structure. St Michael and All Angels was designed by the architect William White, great nephew of the writer and naturalist Gilbert White, and the fabric largely consists of local coloured brick dressed with Bath stone. It took ten years to complete the church.

The West Front, St Michael and All Angels

In the churchyard is the grave of the Hargreaves family who lived nearby at Cuffnells, now demolished. Alice Hargreaves, *née* Liddell, was the inspiration for

Lewis Carroll's *Alice in Wonderland*. She lived at Cuffnells with her husband Reginald for many years. Cuffnells was a large manor house on the outskirts of Lyndhurst, near the *White Swan* on the Christchurch Road. Inside the church you will find a memorial to two of Alice and Reginald's sons, Alan and Leopold, who were both killed in action in the First World War.

The West Door, St Michael and All Angels

If the outside of the church is considered impressive the inside is even more remarkable. The interior is very large and the massive fresco behind the altar is striking. Measuring nearly seven metres wide and two and a half metres high, it is by the Victorian artist Lord Frederic Leighton and depicts the parable of the Wise and Foolish Virgins (*Matthew: Ch.25*). Leighton generously agreed to execute the fresco for only £27 - the cost of the materials - as he was keen to try out a new method of spirit based wall painting that would withstand the English climate. There are also magnificent stained glass windows by the pre-Raphaelite artists William Morris, Edward Burne-Jones and Charles Kempe. Look out for a plaque dedicated to Charles Coleman (and his wife Dinah) who died in 1756 aged 64 and which reads:

Not all the Passions of Mankind
Could shake their uprightness of mind
With Honesty they liv'd and dy'd
And here together they abide.

It is interesting to note that Deputy Surveyor Coleman was in fact removed from office, shortly before he died, for misappropriating large quantities of timber.

In the baptistry is an elaborate marble memorial to Anne Frances Cockerell, *née* Crawford, who died in childbirth aged only 23. Anne lived at The Cottage (later Okefield on the Beaulieu Road) and married a painter and sculptor from London, Samuel Pepys Cockerell who was related to his famous namesake, the diarist, on the distaff side. After his wife's untimely death the devastated Samuel moved back to London to pursue his career. He did not remarry and when he died in 1921 it was his wish to be buried at Lyndhurst with his wife. The churchyard was, by this time, full and although an inscription was placed on Anne's stone Samuel is actually buried in the annexe near Bolton's Bench.

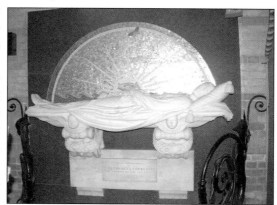

The memorial to Anne Cockerell in the baptistry

The Roman Catholic Church

The church of Our Lady of the Assumption and Saint Edward the Confessor, is situated in Empress Road off the A337 to Cadnam. It is an example of the Early English style of architecture designed by Sir Arthur Blomfield and endowed by Monsieur Edouard Souberbielle.

The entrance to the Roman Catholic Church in Empress Road

Souberbielle was from Tarbes near Lourdes but came to Lyndhurst, sometimes staying at The Cedars, for the hunting. The church is dedicated to the memory of his wife Marie Louise, who died while on one of their visits to the area. There is a plaque to her memory on the outside wall of the church and she is buried in the mausoleum at the east end of the church.

Before the church was built the small Roman Catholic community was served by Father O'Connell who came once a month from Lymington in his pony and trap to a modest building in Wellands Road to celebrate mass. Some members of the congregation travelled from as far away as Totton, Exbury and Fritham to worship there.

The church contains a notable marble floor and mosaics laid by Italian workers brought to England specifically for the purpose. It was built in 1895/6. There are also some fine windows. The west window is dedicated to the men of the 7th Division who left Lyndhurst in 1914 and died in action in Ypres.

Our Lady of the Assumption

The Baptist Church

The oldest church in Lyndhurst is the Ebenezer Baptist Chapel sited, appropriately enough, in Chapel Lane. The present building was constructed in 1848 in the rather severe style of the non-conformists. The gallery was added three years later. The Baptist community in Lyndhurst was already well established by this time with sources suggesting its origins being in the late 17th century - they obtained their first licence in 1689 - and some of the tombstones date from the early 1700s. The chapel record books show a practical and caring approach to the poorer members of the community with frequent entries of sums donated to ease their suffering.

The Baptist Church in Chapel Lane

The chapel can seat a congregation of 150 and its most prominent feature is the pulpit built in memory of Rev T Webb Scammell, minister at the chapel from 1890 to 1928. In the baptistry, below the platform on which the communion table stands, baptisms by total immersion take place. In 2000 a phenomenal fund-raising effort by the fifty or so church members produced enough money, in only six months, to build a new hall. This can be seen behind the church.

One of the more famous members of the Baptist community was the landscape artist Frederick Golden Short, eldest son of the photographers John and Elizabeth Short who ran a chemist's, post office and photographic establishment in the High Street during the second half of the 19th century. Frederick was born and brought up in Lyndhurst and his timeless paintings capture the

The grave of New Forest artist Frederick Golden Short and his sister Emily

spirit of the Forest as few other artists have done, before or since. He was organist at the Chapel for many years and his grave can be found in the grounds. He died in 1936, in his early seventies, having only infrequently, and for short periods, left his beloved New Forest.

Another grave of interest in the grounds is that of Henry Tame, farmer, gardener and lay preacher who lived nearby at Bolderwood. His gravestone states that he died on 2nd February 1900 aged 103 years and 11 months. The story goes that when he reached his 100th birthday he had a pair of boots made but complained to the cobbler that they were too thin and wouldn't last!

Christ Church, Emery Down

This church, three quarters of a mile to the west of Lyndhurst was built in the Early English style in 1864, at a cost of £1200. It was designed by

William Butterfield, is constructed of red Cornish brick and, like the Parish Church, dressed with Bath stone. The church, and the pictur-esque almshouses a short distance away on the opposite side of the road, were the gift of Emery Down's greatest benefactor, Frederick Moore Boultbee (1798-1876). An admiral in the Royal Navy, Boul-tbee retired to Emery Down in 1863 living in a thatched cottage that had once been the village inn called the *Running Horse.*

The almshouses at Emery Down

A plaque in the church commemorates another centenarian, Mark Lovell who died in 1932 aged 103. Another example, perhaps, of the Forest air bestowing longevity on its inhabitants. In the church-yard is a large memorial to Baron Moulton of Bank. This was the brilliant mathematician, lawyer (later Judge) and MP, Sir John Fletcher Moulton (1844-1921), who lived at Forest Green, Bank. He was a friend and neighbour of the novelist Mary Braddon and when he was created a Life Peer in 1912 he took the name of his adopted village as his title.

The lych gate Christ Church, Emery Down

This little church's domestic atmosphere and magnificent setting - the church was built on Forest land granted by the Crown - make a visit here especially memorable. George Tweedie, writing about Emery Down in his book *Hampshire's Glorious Wilderness: Some Rambles and Reflections in and about the New Forest* in 1925, sums up the area perfectly:

"Here by the church a halt should be called, and the little hill climbed for the sake of the exceptionally fine view of rolling woods which is revealed from its summit. These beautiful, far-reaching vistas are ever the despair of the photographer, only his brother of the brush can hope in any degree to bring to the eye its elusive beauties."

Silver Street, Emery Down

22

Chapter Four

Inns and Hospitality

L yndhurst's origins as the seat of New Forest government must have been reflected in its hostelries. Whilst the king and his immediate friends may have been provided for at New Forest lodges the remainder of the retinue of visiting huntsman and officials would have required a bed and sustenance elsewhere. Tracing accurate records from the medieval period though proves problematic. Evidence is more forthcoming in later centuries in which some of the present public houses have their beginnings.

Many pubs would have brewed their own beer in former times but by the early part of the 19th century William Lainson supplied a number of premises with beer from his brewery at The Orchards in Shrubbs Hill Road. He combined this with occasional work as a Forest Regarder, whose duties required him to check and measure felled timber. Unusually perhaps, for a brewer, it is also recorded that his wife offered accommodation to visitors as early as 1810. Apart from the major inns there seemed plenty of choice at this time, for rooms over the shops, described as 'small close', were available as well as more spacious ones a little way from the main street.

The Old Inns

In the 17th century a government survey showed there to be accommodation for twelve people and eight horses in the village. Three inns were recorded in 1676. The *Swan*, which was on Crown copyhold land and run by James Baber, the *King's Arms* under a Mr Freeman and another, unnamed one, which may well have been the *Fox & Hounds*, with a Mr Waterman as the landlord.

Date on the Crown Hotel

When the Heralds (genealogists) visited the Forest ten years later they asked those wishing to establish ancestry to bring proof to the *Kings Arms* between 25th and 27th July. The name of this hostelry disappears from the records after this date. In its place is the *Crown,* perhaps indicating a change of name with the accession of a Queen, Anne, to the throne.

By the 18th century the *Crown* was well established as the place where much Forest business was done. It was once customary for the seller to treat the purchaser on the completion of a bargain. John Wild, as landlord of the *Crown,* received the substantial sum of £7 5s 6d for supplying food and drink after two sales held in December 1769. Local timber dealers were the main recipients of this government hospitality. The Keepers and other Forest officers also received a generous treat once a year at the inn. At one time the fuel allowance for the Verderers and Forest officers was delivered to the inn rather than the Verderers Hall across the road. It certainly is acknowledged in the accounts of the time as receiving good business on Court days. By 1850 even one of the Verderers' Court days was described as 'more like a fair than a judicial court'. With the Church opposite, it was also natural that the sacramental wine should be obtained from the *Crown*.

The Crown Hotel was rebuilt c 1896/7 more than a decade after the Crown buildings to the right were erected. The latter are worth comparing with the parade of shops at the eastern end of the High Street adjacent to the Lyndhurst Park Hotel

Churchwardens' accounts indicate that bell ringing was thirsty work. Not everybody was happy with the service: 'rough waitress, poorly managed Inn' was the comment of diarist William Allingham after a breakfast at the *Crown* in July 1866. In the face of increasing competition for the bottom end of his trade John Palmer employed Joseph Jennings to run a 'tap' in 1881. Extended a number of times as trade increased, the last major rebuild was in 1896/7 when Mrs Mary Jones was the Hotel keeper. Both coaches and horse drawn omnibuses (for Lyndhurst Road Station) stopped here, as do modern buses.

This view of the Fox & Hounds shows little external change in a century apart from the street furniture. Compare with illustration p 54

The *Fox & Hounds* had one of the increasingly rare Forest rights, that of estovers or fuel wood. Considered a nuisance to administer, many of this type of right have been purchased by the Crown over the last two hundred years. The right indicates that there was a building on the site from the beginning of Elizabeth I's reign. Until the 17th century the fuel was collected by the occupier for use in the property with the right. Abuse led to allocation based on previously accepted amounts. Sadly, only one property in Lyndhurst retains this right. The right to six loads, which the inn had, indicates either a large property or the greater quantities required, typical of a pub brewing its own beer. Along with the *Crown* it was the main coaching inn and seems to have thrived with the advent of the turnpike era in the late 18th century. Serving girls were young then, as now, and pay was low. Teenager Sarah Ledge, born in Minstead, came to work for Mr Redford at the *Fox & Hounds* around 1800 for three years, receiving £5 per annum. With greater experience she was then taken on at the *Crown* by John Roblin for 8 guineas (£8.40) for eighteen months.

Most inns have numerous stories attached to them, one of the more gloomy tales concerns the ghost of John Ives, landlord of the *Fox & Hounds* from around 1850 until New Years Day 1867. He had an injured leg and, after falling into the kitchen fire whilst alone, died of his burns and shock during the following night. Strange happenings have been recorded by subsequent tenants of the pub as recently as the 1990s when, around Christmas and New Year taps have been found running and lights flickering. A F Tschiffely whose journey through rural England on horseback was described in *Bridle Paths* (1936), enjoyed staying '*in a delightful old-fashioned inn, the "Fox and Hounds"*'. He had lived in the village twenty years earlier and so enjoyed chatting with the landlord, Charles White, about mutual acquaintances from the 'old days'.

The origins of the name are unknown

The White Swan, sometimes known as the *Swan Inn*, on the outskirts of the village on the Christchurch road, had its uses for those who wished to meet and discuss matters that were not for the ears of officers of the Crown. As with many publicans the landlord doubled as a carrier to Southampton. For the first twenty years of the 20th century John Barnes was the publican who ran the Pony Fair in his yard.

Forest Law kept a strict eye out for unlicensed alehouses. There was al-

26

ways official concern that such places would harbour illegal hunters of the king's game. Following the demise of the Forest system after the 17th century a number of pubs sprang up around the edge of the village. Many more arose following a change in licensing laws in the 1830s. Some inns, such as the *Rising Sun,* the *White Hart* (18th century) and the *New Inn* at Bolton's Bench (*c*1800) run by Joseph Peckham, have come and gone long ago. The *Rising Sun* was run by John Veal in Silver Street, Emery Down in 1849. Many of his relations lived in the same street, a line of forest encroachments, and worked as charcoal makers. There was no lack of choice for thirsty workers, for, just around the corner at the entrance to Northerwood House, John Young was offering beerhouse facilities five years earlier. Others have appeared and disappeared in more recent times.

Both the *Stag* and the *Mailmans Arms* in the High Street started out as beer houses and managed to make the transition to recognized inns offering facilities for locals and tourists alike. William Brixey, a cooper and brewer, ran the beer house that became the *Stag Hotel* for

a couple of decades before passing it on to David Ruffell in the 1860s. It thrived under him and his successor, George Harris. A keen cricketer, by the 1870s Harris was providing accommodation as well as offering dinners for 'Cricket and other Parties'. To meet the demands of increased trade it was enlarged

The Stag's fine facade boasts the date of renovation

and renovated in 1907. Jesse Sevel Newman ran the *Mailmans Arms* in 1871 but was a grocer four years later and then switched to ironmongery before becoming a mail contractor at the end of the decade. In the meantime Frederick Pike who had previously run the *New Forest Inn* took over the *Mailmans Arms* whilst also continuing his trade as a carpenter. William Dove, a whitesmith who lived at the neighbouring Rose Cottage, took it on thereafter - it is his name that is seen above the door in early photographs.

This board outside the Stag Hotel provides a brief note of its origins

The *Volunteer Arms* also started out as a beer house though with relatively few proprietors. Edmund Rogers ran it in the 1870s before it came into the Soffe family where it remained until Montague

Owen Poole took it on in the mid 1920s. Although it ran for many years after this it did not survive into the 21st century and is now used as offices for an estate agent. Its name probably reflects its purpose in helping to quench the thirst of a huge military influx in the Forest in late Victorian times.

The Volunteer Arms is now an office

Outlying Inns

Although many of the present Lyndhurst pubs are not particularly old (as inns go 150 years is a drop in a barrel) they were often housed in old Forest cottages. The *Waterloo Arms* at Pikes Hill may well have started life as a beer house. Its length implies a cottage with, perhaps, a barn attached; ale replacing animals. The attractive, thatched building is probably 18th century and is likely to be much older than the business it contains. Humphrey Collins was the landlord 150 years ago and may have been the first publican. The families of Maynard, Veal and Broomfield were also associated with this pub in the 19th century.

The right hand side of the Waterloo Arms appears to have been the main dwelling

The *Crown Stirrup* formerly the *Crown and Stirrup* at Clay Hill was noted by John Wise in his travels from Brockenhurst in 1861. Although unlikely to have operated before 1835 the building is worth investigating for it seems to be much older. No doubt like many another Lyndhurst business it would not, at first, have provided all the income for the family that ran it. John Shelley had it in 1875 before Ann and Charles Pack. By 1881 Lewis Shepherd, a carpenter, was there with his wife Annie.

The Crown Stirrup at Clayhill. The upstairs windows appear to be Georgian

Emery Down seems to have had more than its fair share of buildings which changed use according to the needs of the times. A hostelry called *The Running Horse* was operating around 1790; in later days this site became the vicarage! The origins of The *New Forest Inn,* still operating in Emery Down, are believed to be a caravan. It is claimed that the older part of the building, to the right, close to the entrance, is based upon this. Glance to the left of the entrance as well to see, on the flat roof, a chaff cutter used to make gorse more palatable for Forest stock. James Pidgeon was the publican at the *New Forest Inn* in the 1870s and 80s and managed to combine this with the job of postmaster.

Forest hospitality at all the inns seems to be a common feature. John Moore recalled a visit to the area in the early 1930s in his book *The*

New Forest. Although he was staying in one of the High Street inns he spent a pleasant evening imbibing in one of the pubs in a hamlet close by. He learnt much from his local darts companion about Forest terms, but whether the short cut back to the centre of Lyndhurst, via a '*hat*' (hill top trees) and a '*shade*' which he took to be a pond (it is actually a pony gathering spot), was accurately remembered is doubtful in his 'relaxed' state.

The New Forest Inn at Emery Down

Chaff Cutter above The New Forest Inn

The central, wooden section of the Inn

Chapter Five

Schools

Prior to the introduction of the state system, schooling was something of a hit and miss affair in many villages. For many it depended on the wealthy for an endowment, often some sort of legacy left in a will. In 1725 two schools were recorded in the parish. One had twenty four girls who were '*cloathed yearly by Her Grace the duchess dowager of Bolton*'. Charles, 3rd Duke of Bolton was Lord Warden of the New Forest at the time. William Phillips in 1787 left funds for a school as well as towards Baptist preaching. This school, attached to the present Baptist Church was still in existence one hundred years later but appears to have closed in 1893.

National and Church Schools

Community interest in education was evident in the early years of the 19th century. It is known that a church (later national) school was started in the King's House around 1817. Initially they met in the Hall before being demoted to the kitchen. The first master, John Smith, was a tailor by trade and already much involved in parish work being clerk as well as churchwarden. The rector, J C Compton, drummed

up pupils by visiting local households. The costs were met by means of a subscription. The pay was scanty by modern standards: £20 a year in the 1820s with an assistant being allowed a mere 4s (20p) a week. By the 1830s

Lyndhurst Infant School. The main building nearest the road was at one time the boys school

girls were being taught by Sarah Carpenter. In 1866 when James Hill was appointed, pay had risen to £47 per annum plus the 'school pence' - pupils' attendance fees.

Following government interest in schooling from the 1830s major improvements were made. Grants were available for building and land owners were encouraged to make land available. This led to the present school site being used following demolition of what had been the King's Stables next to the *Crown Hotel*. The Stables had been turned into barracks during the Napoleonic War and with the demise of the old Forest system under the Lord Warden there was little need for such a large complex. A purpose built school was erected in 1849. In 1881 the Government (as major land holders in Lyndhurst) and Parish exchanged land which enabled further expansion. After extension the school was able to cater for 200 mixed pupils and 100 infants. Although the numbers grew the average attendance by the turn of the century was 140 for the mixed section and 79 for the infants. Fees (the school penny) were removed for elementary education in 1891.

A third school attached to the Plymouth Brethren movement was in existence by 1838, just eight years after the movement came to England. This occupied land in the triangle between Shrubb's Hill Road and Chapel Lane. On its closure in October 1879 the pupils transferred to the National School.

The school at Emery Down was part of the National School at Lyndhurst. Land of nearly a quarter of an acre, 'part of the uninclosed waste of the New Forest', was granted by the Commissioners of Woods in 1859 to the Rector and Churchwardens of the parish. As one of the latter was Lawrence Cumberbatch who also happened to be Deputy Surveyor of the New Forest (and therefore employed by the Commissioners) it is little wonder that the grant was made. The school opened in the early part of 1865 and remained until 1950. For a time after that part was used for the offices of the Verderers. It is now a private house. The Commissioners of Woods made an ad-

The Old School House at Emery Down

ditional free grant of land in 1885 to the Trustees of the school and at the same time granted them a similar parcel of land at Bank for a school.

The Old School Hall in Empress Road was originally a Roman Catholic School. Built into the right hand gate post is one of the last Victorian Postboxes c 1900

Roman Catholics also received separate education prior to the building of their own school, which opened in April 1900, with space for 82 children. Built on land next to the church it has had many uses since its closure in 1934. It was a labour exchange for fifteen years but its main use as a church hall is reflected in the present name. It has been a private house for the last twenty years.

Private Schools

A number of private schools were also offering places in Lyndhurst. Perhaps the best known, and largest, was Parkhill established by Willingham Franklin Rawnsley around 1890. In 1901 it was attended by 15 pupils aged from 9 to 13, many of whom hailed from London. A year or so later Rawnsley left and the school was taken on by Charles Edward Ridout, who advertised it as a preparatory school for Eton. By 1920 it had closed and the building reverted to private use. Retired diplomat Sir Stephen Leech made improvements and lived there until his death in 1925. Later it was transformed into a hotel which it remains, apart from an interruption during the second world war when it was used for military purposes. Author and traveller A F Tschiffely's first teaching appointment was at Parkhill before he moved on to Malvern and eventually Buenos Aires.

Four other schools were advertising for pupils in an 1891 directory. The most prestigious sounding was Herr Metz's 'The New Forest Grammar School (International)' which offered boys 'especial advantages from a health point of view'. Fees for boarders were 40 guineas per annum whilst those for day pupils started at 10 guineas. It was situated at 3, The Custards. The house still stands. It is now a private dwelling but the words 'Grammar School' can still be clearly seen on the side of the building. Signs of its demise as a school may be seen from the fees four years later of seven guineas per term for boarders and a single guinea per term for day pupils that Charles Trodler the new professor of music was offering. Unusually the back of the house is on the road with the front facing the racecourse. It appears to have been purpose built at this time and included a 'good gymnasium and recreation ground'. Free violin or piano lessons were offered to pupils showing talent in these areas. Prior to its move to The Custards the school was operating from Queens Road where Professor Metz had three pupils boarding with him and his assistant teacher Joseph Andrews.

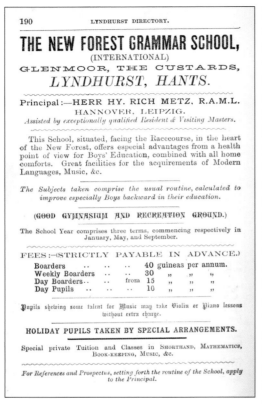

Advertisement from Stevens' 1891 Directory of Lymington and Neighbourhood

Edward Hammick an elementary schoolmaster, who hailed from the west country and could turn his hand to organ tuning, also gave private lessons at his home, Forest Cottage. He was master of the National School for around three decades with his wife running the girls section for much of that time. Mary Soul of The Laurels in Wellands Road offered private schooling and rather oddly her daughter, also Mary, advertised for pupils from an address in the High Street. Both are likely to have been using this to supplement their income.

Mrs Henry Holley appears to have been more successful. She ran a 'High School for Girls' which seems to have started around 1895 when she moved to Queens Road with her builder husband. Although she only had one boarder pupil in 1901, Lucy de Fer from Paris, it is likely that the premises were small and day pupils were her main source of income. She sought to make use of her position by offering extra classes for visitors and was still operating in 1911.

A much more recent school at Clayhill, close to Foxlease, is Coxlease. Opened twenty years or so ago this independent special needs school operates in one of the best kept secrets in Lyndhurst. High Coxlease house was built for Thomas Eustace Smith in 1901 by the architect W R Lethaby in thirty acres of woodland. Lethaby worked for Norman Shaw and was described by Pevsner as '...perhaps Shaw's most brilliant follower...' The house, two storied, is H-shaped and of whitewashed brick with a tiled roof. Smith, who is not known to have local connections, was a Northumbrian ship repairer and a Member of Parliament for Tyneside from 1868 to 1885. He had been staying at Annesley House, Bank when he obtained permission from the land owner, the Crown, to build. There were interesting stipulations in the 99 year lease; the first that at least £4000 should be expended on the house and the second that it should be completed and occupied by 1st October 1901. Whether this was because of Smith's age, he would be seventy by that date, remains a matter of conjecture. In the event the building was completed pretty much on schedule and he lived to enjoy it for just two years.

The south face of High Coxlease House bears the date of completion - 1901

Chapter Six

Sport and Recreation

Hunting

Premier amongst sports in and around Lyndhurst over the centuries has been hunting. William the Conqueror set up the New Forest around 1079 as a sanctuary where he might follow his interests. The Anglo-Saxon Chronicle records that 'he loved the stags as though he had been their father'. It evolved into somewhere he might take his friends hunting and where later kings accorded various privileges making them Masterkeepers of Bailiwicks or sub-divisions of the Forest. In time some of them gained permission to build mansions including those of Rhinefield, Bolderwood and Ironshill. All have now gone though remnants and underkeepers lodges still stand in some parts.

Part of the Old Park bank above Pondhead on the Matley Ridge

A number of Kings' Lodges were set up for the convenience of the visiting monarch. The Queen's House has its origins in this era as well as others at Bolderwood and Queens Bower near Brockenhurst. The most obvious reminder of medieval hunting practice is the remains of the Old Park. This is best seen a mile or so south of the village on the Beaulieu road near Pondhead. The earliest records of fox hunting date from the 16th century when parish authorities paid so much a head for foxes as vermin. Fox hunting on an organised basis dates from 1781 when Vincent, son of Edward Gilbert a Deputy Surveyor of the Forest, started the New Forest Hunt. This added to the already busy hunt scene with rival packs vying for space. The Lord Warden was forced to intervene and settle the days on which various packs would be allowed on to the Forest. Of all the packs the visitors from Goodwood, the Duke of Richmond's pack, took precedence. Not only did others have to give way but this pack was permitted to use the Kennels and Stables at Lyndhurst, and the Duke the King's House.

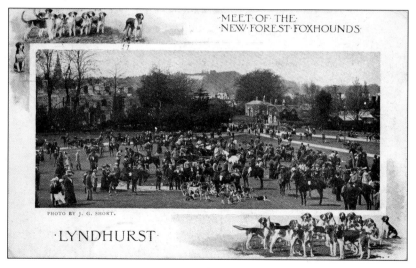

This attractive card, made by John Short in or before 1905, was one of many he and his wife, Elizabeth produced to record great detail of the area

In Victorian times it became popular to spend April in the Forest where the season extended longer than in other parts of the country.

Meets occurred regularly around Lyndhurst at the Queen's House, and 'The Bench' (Bolton's Bench) saw some of the largest fields ever assembled in the New Forest. Officially the Deer Removal Act of 1851 provided a total cull, but in practice animals moved in from outside to fill the vacant stands. This was recognised by, amongst others, Francis Lovell of Hincheslea who hunted deer unofficially from 1858 until 1883. Squabbling over days and areas between his pack and those of the Foxhounds led to official recognition in 1883.

Local hunting practice of a no less barbarous kind was squoyling in which gangs of youths or young men used to throw shaped pieces of wood to bring down squirrels from the trees. A weighted stick, called a squoyle or squog, was the instrument used and in the hands of an expert could bring down the squirrel from a considerable height. Such hunts used to take place between Boxing Day and New Year with the results baked in a pie which I am assured made the effort worthwhile. Red squirrel numbers were decreasing in the early part of the 20th century which hastened the end of this 'sport'. Perhaps former Deputy Surveyor, Gerald Lascelles, best describes attitudes to sport at this time in his book *Thirty-five years in the New Forest* published in 1915:-

> *"But I think the New Forest management has always been lenient in its control and friendly to sports that did no real harm, and sportsmen of all classes, from the highest to the lowest, have ever found it to be a happy hunting ground."*

One of the stranger sights of Lyndhurst, throughout the thirty five years that Gerald Lascelles held the post of Deputy Surveyor at the Queen's House, was young falcons circling the church spire. From his youth Lascelles was a devout falconer and for over forty years was manager of the Old Hawking Club, the only one in England. Although the birds were not usually 'flown' in the Forest their 'Mews' were at the Kings House. Part of their training took place in a corner of Northerwood Park, at the time a home of Lord Londesborough, who was also a member of the Club. Young birds gaining strength were allowed a little liberty in July and August, and became a popular sight with tourists. Aided by a falconer, Lascelles did much of the training of the birds on the racecourse. The Club generally met on Salisbury Plain and the birds were flown over the Wiltshire downs, in the days before the Army took over the area.

Fields below Northerwood House would have been ideal for use by Lascelles and his falconer. The attraction of the spire for the young birds is clear

Racing and the Pony Fair

Horse and pony racing has also been a regular feature of Lyndhurst life. Located on open heathland east of the Cadnam road, the racecourse provided an attractive setting for local competitions. The natural excitement of such a day turned to controversy on some occasions. On one famous occasion, in September 1798, an ox ran a time trial over the course and was said to have completed it 'in such a stile as would not have disgraced an old hunter'. Very much a fair day, the event also encompassed what is generally termed 'rural sports'. School authorities gave in to the inevitable and were in the habit of allowing a holiday on such occasions. The races had a chequered history, restarted in 1858 after a lapse of more than ten years they were still going strong in 1871, when a crowd of four to five thousand attended the days festivities. Although there was some disturbance amongst the bookmakers, upset at one result in particular, there seems no clear reason why the races should have ceased at this time. By 1885 a newspaper account of a sports day shows it to consist mainly of athletic activity and refers to it taking place on the old race course. One story relates that a spoilsport stole the trophy for the main event and the races were never held again.

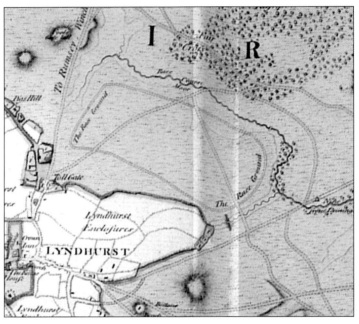

The Race Course, shown on a map of 1789, stretched from the Romsey Road to the Southampton Road

Pony sales took place at a fair held on Swan Green. These were inaugurated by cattle dealers Isaac Trowbridge, Henry Davis and Henry Cheater around the 1840s. They continued in the yard of the *Swan Inn*, with other attractions held on the green opposite. In the last year on the site, 1921, the largest fair ever included steam roundabouts, shooting galleries and swing boats which kept villagers amused well into the night. Elizabeth Broomfield recalled the fair which was usually held on August 9th:

'Bartlett's roundabouts, often two of them, stalls selling ginger-bread and sweets (the stall lady, hearing we had a parrot, used to put aside a bag of nuts for us), hoop-las, Aunt Sally, shooting galleries with balls bobbing in jets of water, swinging boats, coconut shies and always water-squirts...'

George Goddard's view of the Pony Fair in the 'Illustrated London News', 1871

The move to the Race Course was made the following year for safety reasons because of the increase in road traffic and was managed for the first time by The New Forest Pony Association and The Burley and District Pony and Cattle Association. In 1937 after the two so-cieties merged the new chairman, Sir George Meyrick was quoted by Sir Berkeley Pigott as wanting nothing to do with the fair:-

'It serves the Commoners no useful service now. More than half the ponies brought to the fair were not New Forest ponies but Gypsy ponies. There were very few ponies in any case and the whole thing was just a fun fair.'

The Verderers, who managed the fair in 1938 and 1939, were intent on running it in 1940 as late as July of that year before giving way to the inevitable difficulties of war time.

The newly formed pony society took on organisation of pony sales which were transferred to their present location at Beaulieu Road. The racecourse now provides the setting for a golf course. Originally it was set up for locals as a small Forest nine hole 'links' type on the south side of the Southampton Road. It now provides 18 holes in an outstanding setting with good facilities.

Football and Cricket

Although a Football Green has existed in the neighbouring village of Minstead for over two hundred years it is not known how long the game has been played in Lyndhurst. There was certainly a club in existence in 1885. At one time the pitch was behind the High Street at the end of Wellands Road but the area has been used for housing and it is now located further north though still approached through the same road.

Cricket in Lyndhurst has a long history and the village provides one of the most delightful settings in the country for the game. Pitches at Swan Green and Bolton's Bench remain popular but one which was in use at Bank, between the wars, has now been let back to the Forest. The game is known to have been played at Bolton's Bench in the first half of the 19th century. The earliest team seemed to be the New Forest Club drawing many of its members from the larger houses in the village. By 1891 there were two clubs, the Lyndhurst and the New Forest, using this pitch. With the demise of the great days of the large house the former was eventually disbanded. There has been formal permission by the Forestry Commission and their predecessors to use the site since 1888 when the present pavilion was built. There are many stories of the New Forest Club using cricketers of County standard from time to time. Charity matches have been organised against County elevens on a number of occasions. Great inter-war players that enjoyed their cricket at the Bench include Phil

Mead, Stuart Boyes and 'Lofty' Herman. In more recent times perhaps the match that drew the largest crowd, estimated at 3,000, was in 1962 for the Hampshire County Centenary Fund. It must have provided a wonderful day for locals (who somehow included England's Jim Laker amongst their number) to have a chance to match their skills with the County Champions of the previous year.

Cricket at Swan Green seems to have started on the same informal basis as at Bolton's Bench, but a little later. Lord Londesborough of Northerwood House started a club for his friends and family in the 1880s and had the pitch specially made. It was used in the 1890s by a village team organised by Major Ward Jackson from which the present Swan Green Cricket Club has grown. For a brief time in the 1920s there was a name change to Emery Down CC but this was objected to by the then incumbent of Northerwood House, Captain Trinder who would only continue as President if the name reverted. He wanted nothing to do with the name or people of Emery Down as residents in Silver Street had thrown rubbish onto his land!

Sunday Cricket at The Bench

Informal games may have preceded this in a field belonging to the Maxwells of Annesley at Bank. Many of the same names appear including the butcher, John Wiltshire who was known to have, perhaps not surprisingly, a 'tremendous swipe'. The bowler, Bert Pearce used to infuriate his opponents by bowling grass cutters which William Maxwell called 'contemptible things'. However they worked as Pearce said " ..they 'ops an' 'ops, an' 'ops, an' 'as 'em."

Swan Green, Cricket and Pub

Modern Sports

Many of the old pursuits are still practised including Hunting which draws interest from all parts of society from Commoners to the 'Landed Gentry' and plays a part in the Forest economy. Cricket remains popular with the Swan Green and the Lyndhurst Club each playing on at least two days a week throughout the summer. Golf and Football are well established, too, around the village and have been joined by Tennis, Bowls and numerous indoor pursuits, many of them based at the Community Centre. Orienteering is a thriving sport with a number of clubs on the edge of the Forest competing regularly. Ramblers and runners also enjoy their form of relaxation in the local woods with a number of events throughout the year. Cycling is popular with a number of quieter roads in the vicinity and a network of cycle routes not far away.

Walking and horse riding are perhaps the simplest and best ways to see the Forest from Lyndhurst. There are a number of establishments catering for the latter in the area. Walking with a map, or without for those with a love of exploration, is an ideal way to see the old woods.

Peace and quiet, even on the busiest of public holidays may be found little more than half a mile from the Forest car parks. Lyndhurst, totally surrounded by the Crown Lands, is a near perfect centre for this exploration.

One of the many cycle tracks near Lyndhurst

Natural History

Natural history pursuits have been a major objective of many visitors in the last 130 years. In the 1880s and '90s James Gerrard and George Tate offered their services as entomologists providing expertise and local knowledge. The aim in those days, the capture of specimens, is no longer acceptable. The decline and, in a few cases total absence of species, is in part due to this practice. The mild southern climate and diversity of habitats, however, enable visitors to the New Forest to observe many species of wildlife scarce in other areas.

A mile or so south of the village along the Brockenhurst road, the first Forest car park on the left, Clayhill Heath, provides the nearest access to the recently named Frohawk Ride. F W Frohawk was an artist and entomologist whose twenty four year pioneer study of the life cycle of butterflies provided the basis for modern understanding of the subject. Numerous visits to the New Forest with his family provided him with much of his material. The ride, away from graz-

The ride named after F W Frohawk near Clayhill

ing stock, providing breeding grounds for a number of species, was formally named by his daughter Valezina (herself named after a butterfly!) in 1996.

Deer may be seen at any time or place in the Forest, usually away from people but occasionally in gardens. The easiest way to observe them in daylight is by taking a trip to Bolderwood where a platform at the Deer Sanctuary enables comfortable viewing.

To the west of the village on the Christchurch Road just beyond Allum Green there is a Forest track leading to the reptiliary. Here, at least in the warmer months, may be seen most of the Forest's snakes, toads, frogs and newts.

Not all naturalists appreciated Lyndhurst and all that it had to offer.

W H Hudson who, perhaps, was more of an observer than a collector, delivered this polemic in his book *Hampshire Days*, first published a century ago:

> *"Lyndhurst is objectionable to me not only because it is a vulgar suburb, a transcript of Chiswick or Plumstead in the New Forest where it is in a wrong atmosphere, but also because it is the spot on which London vomits out its annual crowd of collectors, who fill its numerous and ever-increasing brand-new red-brick lodging-houses, and who swarm through all the adjacent woods and heaths, men, women, and children (hateful little prigs!) with their vasculums, beer and treacle pots, green and blue butterfly nets, killing bottles, and all the detestable paraphernalia of what they would probably call "Nature Study."*

Damselfly

Song Thrush egg on beech leaves

Heath Spotted-orchid

Chapter Seven

Commoners, Characters and Change

Occupation and industry in Lyndhurst has for centuries been based on timber and services. Lord Wardens have run the Forest from medieval times until the mid 19th century. Accounts of the steward to one in the 18th century, the Duke of Bedford, show lists of local people employed in a variety of ways. Some people were involved in traditional farming occupations, others, both craftsmen and labourers, were making repairs to Crown property. When the Lord Warden or other important guests were staying at the King's House there was much service work to be done. Those employed ranged from carpenters, plumbers, glaziers, smiths and basket workers through to traders supplying linen and foodstuffs. There were, of course, many employed in providing direct labour for cleaning, cooking, taking messages and transporting materials. These occupations would have been just as necessary in the 13th century as in the 18th. Secretarial services may have grown in recent times but the need to make payments and keep accounts was always an important part of any business whether Crown or private.

Forest work

Timber and deer protection have been a major part of the Forest economy. A system of keepers, browsers to feed the deer, and woodmen to protect the inclosures evolved, based in Lyndhurst. When new inclosures were being created for timber production in the 18th century men were required to clear the land, remove the old timber, plant oats (to 'sweeten' the land) harvest and sell it and then sow the acorns or beech mast. Protection from vermin and erection and maintenance of hedges and banks to keep out deer and Forest stock was then important.

In addition to this there was a private but linked timber related industry. Coppice working was the traditional method of using the Forest before timber inclosures were created. This involved the production of 'standards' (timber trees) which would take many decades to reach maturity and underwoods which could be used for a variety of purposes. It was the right to the latter that was sold off to local people who then made anything from hurdles to roof spars with the growth of the young 'poles'. Charcoal making was the way to tidy up the 'refuse' wood that had no other purpose. This might then be used by smiths, for cooking, coastal salt production or even transporting to other areas such as Cornwall for tin smelting.

A Cottage in Silver Street, Emery Down built in 1869 by Henry Veal, shows these intriguing patterns of the Charcoal Makers art

A thriving black market in turning one of the Forest rights - 'estovers' - to cash in hand was by making truck wheels and rails for sale to coal mines in Newcastle. Strictly speaking the right was restricted to a limited number of residences for fuel wood in that house alone. When the administration was lax and times were bad there was no lack of local ingenuity. Even the new inclosures were used as a source of income for irregularly paid keepers by their breeding and selling rabbits. Oddly enough coal mining, or perhaps prospecting, took place in the 17th century on the outskirts of Lyndhurst. Close to Beechen Lane where the road leaves the village there is an area once known as 'Minehouse Grounds' but now part of Pondhead Inclosure.

One of the main means of support for many people in Lyndhurst was stock rearing. The Forest provides opportunity for the grazing of more cattle and ponies than could be kept on a small holding. Although likely to have been only a part of the income of most households it none the less kept regular money coming in through the sale of butter and milk. Pigs turned out in the autumn not only reduced the supply of beech mast and acorns which could, in excess, poison ponies but in the process fattened themselves. Many a young Commoner, given a pig to turn out, learnt an important lesson in economics by 'adding value' during this pannage period.

Pigs at pannage at Hurst Hill south of Lyndhurst

As the popularity of Lyndhurst grew in the 18th and 19th centuries, with more and more large houses being built, the need for domestic staff increased. Whilst a number of estates were only used in the hunting season, with a large permanent retinue brought down from elsewhere, there was still some temporary employment as well as the use of other local goods and services. This expanded considerably from the mid 19th century onwards when better access through the opening of the railway network enabled more people to travel. Both the old coaching inns, the *Fox and Hounds* and the *Crown,* operated an omnibus service to connect with the station three miles away at Lyndhurst Road (Ashurst).

Perhaps one of the more unusual occupations to be found in a small country village was that of James Hinves who died in 1783. He was a wigmaker who evidently found enough custom amongst the better off members of society to sustain himself. Even less likely was the aptly named Aaron Coster, a fisherman who died in 1737.

Perhaps the clue lies with his contemporary Augustus Grant who was described as 'of Lyndhurst and Newfoundland'. The opportunities in the New World clearly appealed to the Grant family for another member, John, held land there in the same period. Newfoundland at the time had a population of about 2,000 and was little more than a summer fishing ground where the catch could be dried and packed as well as nets repaired apart from giving shelter when needed.

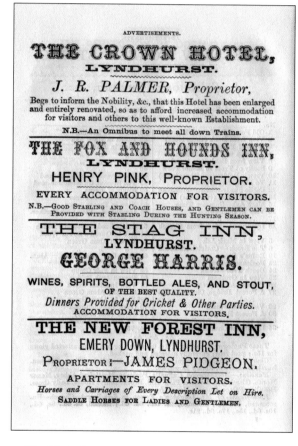

Much of the early accommodation for travellers and visitors was to be found in the inns, but villagers were not slow to offer alternatives as tourism grew in the 18th and 19th centuries. In the early 1800s visitors to the village could choose between small rooms over shops and more spacious ones in cottages set a little way out. Those with connections could stay with friends; some of the larger houses and mansions operated a virtual open house system in the season.

The 1876 edition of Phillips Guide to the New Forest shows the Lyndhurst Inns competing for trade

Apartments and rooms to let grew throughout Victorian times when the Forest first came to be appreciated for its nature conservation and recreational value. Many of those properties offering accommodation today have been welcoming guests for over a hundred years. Adaptability was the key to survival. Pat's Garage in the Romsey road was operating before the war. It had been Robert Rowdon's prior to that, starting out as coach builders in the 19th century.

High Street c 1880 with the Fox & Hounds on the left and George Halfacre's coach building premises second on the right

Snake Catchers - Henry 'Brusher' Mills and George Wateridge

The best known unconventional occupation was that of snake catcher. At least four gentlemen are known to have operated in this 'profession' in the Forest - two of them in and around Lyndhurst. Brusher Mills was born in 1840 at Emery Down, and lived the early part of his life at Silver Street. He started catching and selling snakes to the London Zoological Society around 1880 at 1 shilling (5p) a time. He then lived in the Clayhill area. He chose to live in a disused charcoal makers hut about a mile to the south of this area in Whitley wood, remaining there for 19 years until the hut was burned in 1903. His 1901 census entry of 'New Forest Snake Catcher' must have caused the civil servants of the day some difficulty in categorising him.

Lancelot Speed's illustration 'The Adder-Catcher' showing Henry Mills appeared in Charles Cornish's 'The New Forest' in 1894

One story thought to relate to him concerns his taking a particularly fine specimen to a large house where the owner, pleased with the find, purchased it. Being an invalid he asked Brusher to take it into the next room where he would find a large bottle of alcohol in which to preserve it. A while later the lady of the house found a 'tramp' fast asleep on the sofa; the gardener assisted by the chauffeur removed him to a shed to finish his sleep. A few days later an unpleasant smell was traced to the, by now, decayed snake. Closer inspection revealed the jar had been filled with plain water and the missing alcohol was thus accounted for inside the 'tramp'. Other ways of procuring a penny or two was to quietly drop a snake in amongst a crowd of visitors and after the commotion 'rescue' it. He would then happily receive the thanks directly or by means of a drink, a trick that his successor, George Wateridge, wasn't averse to using.

The nickname 'Brusher' was believed to originate from his time at Clayhill where he worked as a labourer and is thought to have brushed the ice for skaters on the lake in Foxlease Park. Another theory is that it was due to his assiduous clearing of a Forest cricket pitch prior to a game. He did not live entirely in the woods for he still had relatives in Lyndhurst and would appear occasionally for a change of clothes or even a bath. His demise took place in the Railway Inn, Brockenhurst where after a drink or two and a meal he collapsed and died of heart disease and was thus buried in the churchyard of St Nicholas.

George Wateridge of Pondhead took over the work, supplying both London Zoo and the Scottish Zoological Society with specimens. He kept his snakes in a dustbin which, when sufficient numbers had accumulated, he would despatch by means of his children to Lyndhurst Road Station (now Ashurst). He also supplied lizards, toads and frogs to the Zoos, no doubt for feeding purposes. Like Tate and Gerrard before him he was also something of an entomologist. He continued his work, when fit enough to do so, until his death in 1948 at the age of 79. The days of such deeds are over, for catching wildlife in the Forest is now prohibited.

The wide rides of the Forest Enclosures, many of them made in the 19th century, became a Mecca for enthusiastic insect collectors. The long grass, free from the grazing of Commoners stock and with few deer since the Deer Removal Act of 1851, provided a haven for butterflies. James Gerrard was something of a handyman, he advertised himself as a joiner and builder but became an expert entomologist when the opportunity arose.

Growth and Change

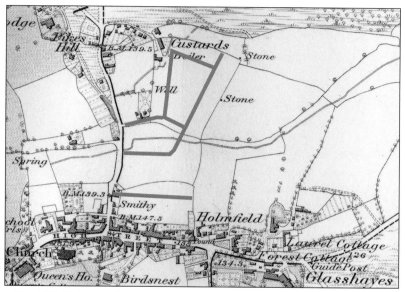

The 1871 Ordnance Survey map shows virtually empty fields north of the High Street and is overlaid here with the roads that were in place by 1897
© *Crown Copyright 1871*

Lyndhurst's position in the centre of the New Forest precluded any large growth or sprawl there until the 19th century. Up until 1800 it remained much the same size as Minstead with a population of under a thousand, having, perhaps, doubled in the previous 100 years. It grew to just over fifteen hundred by mid century but then didn't expand further until the 1880s. The Lyndhurst of the 1870s was described by W Chambers:

"We can hardly imagine a place more primitive. Its few

*shops are of a compound character. The baker deals in
stationery; the grocer sells carpets, and the chemist has
a fair show of drapery and photographs. There is no
bookseller or newsvendor, and no bank for general accommodation in money matters. The town, to call it so,
has no gas-lamps for lighting the thoroughfare. Water
is not laid on to the houses, and there is no system of
sewage. Yet we see nothing offensive..."*

By 1891 it boasted a reading room and working men's club, a brass
band, its own hall with an annual art exhibition, mutual benefit societies and good sporting facilities. Some of the services did not arrive
till the new century but it clearly offered a great deal for visitors
and new residents alike. Expansion started in the 1870s due to the
national publicity surrounding government plans to enclose much
of the Forest for timber plantations and sell off the remainder. An
art exhibition in London in 1875 attracted contributions from both
local and, more importantly, nationally famous artists including the
president and various members of the Royal Academy, which helped
people to appreciate the Forest for its aesthetic qualities and thereby

*The view towards Forest Point and the village from the north showing 19th century
development right up to the forest boundary*

save it. This fresh interest brought visitors keen to understand and see the area for themselves. Artists visited regularly, some came to stay. Stephen Harvey in 1878 advertised himself as a picture framer and naturalist thus covering two of the new found reasons to visit Lyndhurst.

Rapid growth in population to over two thousand took place within the 1890s. Much of the village consisted of Crown manor lands which were sold off from 1850 onwards. This, together with private development, allowed building on areas such as the strangely named Custards between the centre of the village and the golf course. One version of the odd sounding name is that with the police station close by this was where defendants were held in custody: not too likely as the police station was only built in 1969 and the area has had its name for more than 160 years. Custard apple trees growing on the farm that used to stand there is another possibility. A third option is a personal name; perhaps Thomas Costard, a butcher, who died in the village in 1707, and may have held lands there.

Many people were responsible for the development of the village, amongst them was John Maxwell, the publisher husband of Mary Braddon who according to his son was 'an enthusiastic builder'. Apart from their own house, Annesley at Bank, which was added to time and again, several properties in the village bear their mark and owe their existence to his enthusiasm and, perhaps, her success.

The Northerwood estate was sold in the 1890s to Edward Festus Kelly, directory publisher in the family business and descendant of the founder Frederic Kelly. Part of the lands were sold off and allowed, in the words of W H Rogers, *'erection of a number of detached houses, making the area a beautiful miniature 'Garden City,' called 'Forest gardens'*". He went on to say that Pike's Hill *'has changed entirely - the small old houses have been replaced by quite a large number of large new ones, a fine avenue projected, and a 'Children's Hospital' built, by Mr. Fenwick.'* This description of Pikes Hill may be welcome news to present inhabitants for the name is recorded as

'*Pigs Hill*' on a map of 1789, no doubt reflecting its popularity as a pannage area. The hospital was preceded by a convalescent home, also at Pikes Hill, now a private house.

Large Houses

There remains in Lyndhurst a number of houses or mansions, some built or having their origins in the 18th century or before. Many are shrouded in mystery, with the details of their beginnings lost. North-erwood House, built on a ridge close to Emery Down, commands the best views of anywhere in the district. The block of land on which it stands once belonged to the Elcombe family after whom the 17th century house opposite the Queen's House was named. The earliest building seems to have taken its name from a field called Dorehayes. By the mid 18th century a local farmer Richard Gain held land there. A little later Southampton merchant Robert Ballard was in posses-sion. Twice Mayor of Southampton, he held numerous civic posts in the town as well as a number of potentially remunerative ones and seems the most likely originator of the present building.

The south facing facade of Northerwood House

A Forest inquiry in 1801 indicates that Ballard had the site by 1781 and that he was busy building and pushing his boundaries a little too far for the liking of the Crown authorities. It was in his time, 1789, that King George III, who was staying with George Rose at Cuffnells, paid a visit to admire the view and suggested that the house be renamed Mount Royal. The name lasted as long as the King but reverted to Northerwood thereafter. Ballard died in December 1794; shortly afterwards it passed into the hands of Charles William Michell, a gentleman with estates in the West Indies and who had connections with the sugar industry. A guide book of 1844 states that Ballard built the present house, although it is quite clear that it has been added to over the years. Both Michell and his successor John Pulteney made many improvements, the latter's family also setting out the grounds with exotic species. It was let for much of the second half of the 19th century and used by Lord Londesborough as a country seat in the hunting season.

Foxlease, in its attractive setting and outwardly retaining many of its Georgian features, is an international centre for Girl Guides

Foxlease, to the south of the village is situated in its own park of 65 acres and has been used as a centre for Girl Guides since it was gifted to the Association in 1922. An interesting building, much altered, built in the 18th century it is one of the few large (and not so large) houses to have escaped being turned into a Hotel at some stage in its life. Known at one time as Coxlees the site is believed to be Cocherlei mentioned in Domesday, and then consisting of around 90 acres. It is mentioned in a Forest document of 1604 as being of 120 acres let to a William Brown who paid 13s 4d (67p) in annual rent. The remainder of the document describes the bounds of the Inn (Lyndhurst) Bailiwick which may still be traced today. A Bailiwick was a division of the Forest, the 1604 line is very similar to the present parish boundary. The house, with its doric columns, bears the date 1775, and is believed to have been partly built around a lodge of the 17th century by Sir Phillip Jennings Clerke. The original entrance, past the Coach House at Goose Green, and over the lake became unsafe.

This attractive sign marks the old entrance to Foxlease

Vernalls, another house of some age and character used to stand near Goose Green. This was the home of Arthur Phillip in the 18th century. He was a naval man who married and settled in Lyndhurst at Vernalls around 1763. His house has long since been replaced but the farm of the same name still stands. On the outbreak of hostilities with France he volunteered for service again and in 1786 received the call to form a convict settlement in Australia. He worked hard in preparation and sailed with the first fleet in 1788. His accomplishment, as first Governor and founder of Sydney, in putting over 1700 acres under cultivation in extremely difficult conditions, made the colony self sufficient.

Chapter Eight

The Arts in Lyndhurst

L yndhurst has attracted writers, artists and musicians by the score over the centuries. The well known novelist Fanny Burney (1752-1840) visited Lyndhurst in the royal entourage of George III. In 1789, she wrote:

> *"The New Forest is all beauty, and when we approached Lyndhurst the crowds wore as picturesque an appearance as the landscapes; they were all in decent attire, and, the great space giving them full room, the cool beauty of the verdure between the groups took away all idea of inconvenience, and made their live gaiety a scene to joy beholders."*

The royal party stayed at the King's House. On the first night of the monarch's stay, while he was dining at King's House, the crush of the crowd broke the fencing and hedges in their efforts to observe the king at table. Fanny was Second Keeper of the Robes to Queen Charlotte and experienced a freedom, during her stay in Lyndhurst, that few women of her class could enjoy.

Another famous visitor in the 18th century was the artist and caricaturist Thomas Rowlandson (1756-1827) who took a post-chaise tour of the south of England in the early 1780's which included a stay in Lyndhurst. He sketched Lyndhurst church and the *Crown Inn* and stables opposite.

The novelist, playwright and composer Catherine Gore (1799-1861) made her home in Lyndhurst for many years as did the song writer and composer Ellen Dickson (1819-1878) better known in her day as "Dolores". Mary Braddon (1835-1915), a 'queen of the circulating library' and author of *Lady Audley's Secret*, built a large house called Annesley at Bank. Mary wrote at least two novels with a New Forest setting, *Vixen* and *Mount Royal*, the old name for Northerwood House. She and her publisher husband John Maxwell were also responsible for several other buildings in Lyndhurst - the Crown buildings in the High Street and Queens Place in Pemberton Road still bear their initials. Oscar Wilde was a frequent visitor to Annesley. When he started to write short stories he would read them to Mary, before publication, for her critical appraisal

Crown buildings in the High Street bear the initials of Mary Braddon and her publisher husband, John Maxwell

In 1886 the New Forest Hall was opened by a cabinet-maker, William Gerrard, on the present site of Budgens Supermarket. It was a large supper and tea rooms but its principle purpose being for "theatricals, concerts and entertainments" of all kinds. It boasted a superbly sprung dance floor and every summer three art exhibitions were held at the Hall. It evolved, in the mid-1930s, into a cinema which flourished until the late 60s. There was also, at the beginning of the 20th

Lyndhurst's only supermarket, Budgens, was once the New Forest Hall, and, for over thirty years, the Plaza Cinema

century, a small but well regarded Art Gallery at the eastern end of the High Street.

Amongst the principal exhibitors at the New Forest Hall and Art Gallery would have been a trio of Lyndhurst artists: John Emms (1841/3 -1912), Arthur Batt (1846-1911) and Frederick Golden Short (1863-1936) all of whom lived and worked in Lyndhurst in the late 19th and early 20th centuries. The young John Emms came to the New Forest to work, under the tutelage of Frederic Leighton, on the famous fresco of the *Wise and Foolish Virgins* in St Michael and All Angels church. Emms was so drawn to the Forest that later he returned and stayed for the rest of his life. He lived in Queens Road, Lyndhurst with his wife Fanny, daughter of the Keeper of Denny Walk, George Primmer. Arthur Batt, born in Whitchurch, came to live and work, first in Lyndhurst and then in Brockenhurst. Frederick Golden Short is Lyndhurst's own famous son. Born and bred in Lyndhurst he had no desire to leave his native area. He was the eldest son of the chemist and pioneer photographers John and Elizabeth Short whose premises were in the High Street. He attended Southampton Art School, which was founded in 1855, and earned his living by painting Forest landscapes. At the age of only eighteen he illustrated a major work, *Autumnal Leaves* by F G Heath. Golden Short's studio was in the High Street.

The novelist Horace Vachell

Arthur Conan Doyle (1859-1930), best known for his creation of the detective Sherlock Holmes, tucked himself away for a year in a tiny cottage at Emery Down while he researched what he considered one of his best novels, *The White Company,* an historical tale which is set in the New Forest. Later he came to live at Bignell Wood, Brook. He is buried in Minstead churchyard.

Another prolific novelist, well known in his day, was Horace Vachell (1861-1955).

Vachell lived in a house on the site of the present day Rufus Court in Gosport Lane and in his novel *The Yard*, which was published in 1923, he calls Lyndhurst "Puddenhurst". This light romance is based around stables in Lyndhurst and the hunting scene. Forest place names are thinly disguised by the alteration of, in many cases, a single letter.

Another author who used Lyndhurst as a setting for one of his books was W E Johns, more famous for his Biggles adventures. The book, a spy tale entitled *Sinister Service*, was published in 1942.

The frontispiece from 'The Yard', a novel set in Lyndhurst, by H A Vachell

The poet, Rupert Brooke (1887-1915), was a regular visitor to Lyndhurst, enjoying the cooking of Mrs Primmer with whom he stayed at Beech Shade, Gritnam near Bank. Virginia Stephen, later Woolf (1882-1941), visited her aunt Sarah Duckworth at Lane End, Bank in the Christmas holidays of 1904 and 1906.

Allum Green, the tiny hamlet on the south-western outskirts of Lyndhurst, was once home to the writer and pacifist Vera Brittain (1893 - 1970). She bought Allum Green Cottage in 1939 with the proceeds of her book, *Testament of Youth*. The cottage is still owned today by Vera's family and often visited by her daughter, the well known politician Shirley Williams.

Today the arts are still flourishing in Lyndhurst. Busy Music and Art Societies meet regularly in the Community Centre and a thriving Drama Group stage performances each year in the Vernon Theatre, Sandy Lane. Angels Farm Pottery, run by professional New Forest potter Joanna Osman, is situated on the junction of Chapel and Pinkney Lanes and is well worth a visit. There is a Picture Shop specialising in New Forest prints, and a Fine Art Café, both in the High Street. The Fine Art Café shows many original paintings and craftwork as well as the incredibly artistic chocolate creations of its owner who is an award winning Chocolatier.

The Bead Gallery in the High Street was once home to the estate agents Sawbridge & Son. The photograph (left) appeared in a guide book published by Sawbridges in 1936, and (right) as it appears today

The Bead Gallery, at the west end of the High Street, is where husband and wife team Celia and Norman Round ply their trade. Celia makes and repairs jewellery and Norman paints in watercolour, oil and pastel.

St Michael and All Angels, of course, offers the artistic gems of its huge reredos fresco and stained glass windows. The New Forest Museum and Visitor Centre, off the main car park, in the centre of Lyndhurst gives an audio-visual presentation of the story of the Forest as well as displays and dioramas. A special feature is the New Forest Embroidery created in 1979 to commemorate the 900th anniversary of the New Forest. The building also houses a New Forest Resource Library, a great boon to local historians and researchers.

Angels Farm Pottery on the junction of Chapel and Pinkney Lanes, and some examples of the work of New Forest potter, Joanna Osman

Angels Farm House, next to the pottery, is one of the oldest houses in Lyndhurst. It is a splendid example of a 17th century lobby-entrance farmhouse

Possibly, the most famous literary connection with Lyndhurst is, for many people, its association with Lewis Carroll's *Alice in Wonderland*. Alice deserves a chapter all to herself...

Chapter Nine

'Alice' in her Wonderland

Lewis Carroll, pseudonym of Charles Lutwidge Dodgson, a mathematical don at Christ Church College Oxford for nearly fifty years, gained immortality as the creator of one of the most famous of all characters in the history of children's literature - Alice. Carroll's life has been well documented and most are probably familiar with the story of how the shy and stuttering young man, who had a passion for photography, came to meet the 'real' Alice for whom the story was written.

Alice Pleasance Liddell was born in 1852, the fourth of the ten children (two died in infancy) of Henry Liddell, who later became Dean of Christ Church. The Dean and his wife befriended the young Dodgson and the children loved him for his ability to enter their world so completely. Dodgson, who was always more comfortable in the company of children, lost his stutter in their presence and never tired of entertaining them with jokes and stories.

On July 4th 1862 Dodgson, then aged thirty, took the young daughters of the Dean, Lorina, Alice and Edith, rowing near Godstow. He began one of his nonsense tales of a little girl who fell down a rabbit hole 'without the least idea what was to happen afterwards'. Alice begged him to write it down for her and the legend was born. The story started life in manuscript form, as *Alice's Adventures Underground* and was not published until three years later, in December 1865, much expanded, and illustrated by Sir John Tenniel, as *Alice's Adventures in Wonderland*.

Tenniel's Alice bore no physical resemblance to Alice Liddell who was dark, always wore a fringe and had haunting good looks. She was, as one might expect of a daughter of the Dean, very well educated, excelling in French, music and painting; she received painting lessons from Ruskin who lent her Turners' sketches to copy. She was educated, indeed, in all the genteel pursuits expected of a lady of her class but without any expectation that they need be used. Alice, taught at home by an army of governesses and tutors, just missed the period of social change when women won the first battle in their long fight to be given the opportunity of an education equal to their brothers. The year before Alice's marriage, the first two ladies' colleges, Somerville and Lady Margaret Hall, were founded.

Many undergraduates at Christ Church must have fancied themselves in love with the attractive daughters of the Dean. It is not known exactly when one of those undergraduates, Reginald Gervis Hargreaves, whose family owned Cuffnells in Lyndhurst, first met Alice, but they became engaged in July 1880. They were married, by special licence, the following September in Westminster Abbey. Alice saw Cuffnells for the first time a week before the wedding and in a letter to Reginald her euphoria is obvious:

> *"After all, I really don't know what to say to you!...I did not say very much to you yesterday, I think, but can you guess a little bit how enchanted I was? I hope it will be a real fairyland to us both as long as we are both permitted to enjoy it, dear; 'Wonderland' come true to 'Alice' at last!"*

Cuffnells was a country seat on a grand scale. Set to the west of the village, in one hundred and sixty acres of land, it had been previously owned by George Rose. Rose was, variously, a New Forest Verderer, MP for Lymington and Christchurch, and a statesman who held several posts in the Exchequer. Besides receiving frequent visits from the Prime Minister, he also entertained King George III and Queen Charlotte on several occasions as they travelled from Weymouth to London. They slept in the 'gold room', a suitably majestic bedroom where all the fittings and furnishings were gold, even down to the coverlet on the four-poster bed. It was Rose who had made the major additions to the house. A drawing-room, measuring twelve and a half by seven metres, and a similar sized dining-room with oval vestibule made up the south front, finished with an impressive orangery over thirty metres long. A balcony ran the length of the upper storey and from the rear were magnificent views over the Solent to the Isle of Wight. There was a large billiard room, a grand staircase and a library.

Cuffnells as it appeared in Brayley and Britton's 'Beauties of England and Wales' in 1805. At this time it was the seat of the Rt Hon George Rose

Reginald's parents, Jonathan and Anna, had acquired the estate in 1856 and enriched the already fine and exotic gardens, creating a 'wilderness' in which their children, Reginald and his two sisters, Fanny and Emma, could play. There was a small lake, suitable for fishing and a rhododendron bush measuring fifty paces round.

Alice and Reginald were happily married for forty six years and brought up a family of three sons at Cuffnells. Reginald was described by his contemporaries as a kindly, gentle man, gregarious and sociable. He was not an academic; he ran the estate and was a keen sportsman and made up with energy and enthusiasm what he lacked intellectually. He was Chairman of the Conservative Club and a JP, eventually becoming senior magistrate of the New Forest Division. He was a member of the parish council and district commissioner of the local boy scouts. Reginald's main preoccupation was cricket. In 1874 he had a cricket pitch laid in the grounds of Cuffnells and many important matches were played there. He later became President of Lyndhurst Cricket Club, the New Forest Cricket Club and then Hampshire.

Alice, used to the society of the leading academic minds of her day was, from all accounts, content. She oversaw the running of the house, a not inconsiderable task in view of its vast size, and became first president of the Emery Down Women's Institute. She organized flower shows and gymkhanas, complete with bands and marquees, which became major events at Cuffnells.

Together they brought up their sons Alan, born in 1881, Leopold, known to the family as Rex, born in 1883 and finally Caryl who arrived four years later. Alan chose a military career and went to Sandhurst from where he joined the Rifle Brigade as a second lieutenant. Rex and Caryl did not make the same choice as their brother but, when the war broke out in 1914, they immediately enlisted, in the Irish and Scots Guards.

Sadly, both Alan and Rex lost their lives in the war, leaving Caryl heir to the estate. Luckily Reginald and Caryl had a lot in common, both enjoying fishing, shooting and golf. They spent a lot of time together in Reginald's last years which must have helped to bridge the enormous gap left by the death of his two eldest sons. Reginald died, at Cuffnells, on St Valentines Day, 1926 at the age of seventy-three and is buried in the

The memorial to Alan and 'Rex' in St Michael's church

family grave in St Michael and All Angels, Lyndhurst.

Caryl didn't marry until he was in his early forties, and gave Alice her only grandchild Mary Jean. Alice lived on at Cuffnells but the enormous house proved too difficult to maintain. Caryl and his wife, Madeleine, spent much of their time in London coming home to Cuffnells only occasionally. Alice took to spending half the year at Westerham in Kent to be near her only surviving sister, Rhoda. This is where she was staying when she was taken ill and died in November 1934, aged eighty-two. She was cremated at Golders Green and her ashes placed next to Reginald in Lyndhurst churchyard.

The Hargreaves family grave in St Michael's churchyard

Alice lived to see her namesake become part of world folklore. *Alice* was translated into many foreign languages, as well as Latin, Braille and even shorthand. Alice's own wonderland, Cuffnells, became a hotel for a short time after her death but it was requisitioned in the Second World War for use by a searchlight battalion. Afterwards its condition was so dilapidated that, with no money for refurbishment, it was demolished.

Chapter Ten

Bank and Allum Green

On the outskirts of Lyndhurst are the hidden treasures of Bank and Allum Green. Both situated a mile or so from the village they can be accessed easily on foot or by car. Taking the A35 road to Christchurch/Bournemouth, once the *White Swan* on the left and Swan Green on the right have been passed, the road climbs towards the open Forest and in a short while there is a turning to the left marked Bank. Prior to the turn it is possible to catch a glimpse, amongst the trees before the cattle grid, of Cuffnell Cottage, a former lodge house to the Cuffnells estate.

Cuffnell Cottage, Bank. Above the door are the initials RGH (Reginald Gervis Hargreaves)

Over the grid the large white house on the left is called Lane End. This is where the young Virginia Stephen, later to become Virginia Woolf, stayed with her Aunt, Sarah Duckworth. Virginia, suffering even in these early years from the depression that was to dog her all her life, found that the Forest air lifted her spirits and she returned to London refreshed and happy.

The Oak Inn, Bank

It is possible to park near the only pub, *The Oak*, and a stroll round the tiny village will be well rewarded. The road to the right of the pub leads, eventually, to the isolated hamlet of Gritnam, but half way along there is a large country house, now apartments, called Annesley. This was the home of Bank's other famous literary lady, Mary Braddon. Mary was a phenomenally successful writer in her day. She founded a magazine, *Belgravia,* and published dozens of sensational novels which dealt with bigamy, blackmail and murder. Mary's private life also caused something of a sensation. She lived openly with her publisher John Maxwell, whose wife was in an asylum for the insane in Ireland. She cared for Maxwell's five children

Annesley, Bank. Once home to the novelist Mary Braddon

as well as six of their own until his wife's death in 1874, after which they married.

A corner at Bank

The road to the left of the pub leads to a scattering of delightful cottage homes: one, near the postbox, carries a date of 1600.

On regaining the A35, still heading towards Bournemouth, and after half a mile or so there is an unmarked turning to the right which leads to the tiny hamlet of Allum Green. The writer and pacifist Vera Brittain, and her husband George Catlin, came to live at Allum Green Cottage at the outbreak of the Second World War. Her diary recalls their first view of the cottage '*We loved it at once; glorious position, right on the edge of the forest...*'. Nearby Allum Green House, once home to George Fenwick, founder of the cottage hospital, was requisitioned for military use in 1940 and by the end of the war had been severely bomb-damaged.

Tucked away in the trees, on a rise, to the south west of the settlement, is a seat with a plaque dedicated to four men - Tyler, Avon, Gifford and Blunn - who were casualties of the bombing.

Prior to 1841 when the turnpike road from Lyndhurst to Christchurch

Memorial seat and plaque at Allum Green

was inaugurated the only good road west from the village was called the Cut Walk starting from the top of Emery Down hill. Running straight for much of its length it is also known as the 'Gun Barrel' by Hardley Runners, a local group who often used to finish their activity by climbing the hill at the Swan Green end.

The road was made at the request of a Lord Warden of the New Forest, Charles, 3rd Duke of Bolton who had property in Burley. Clearly built for his own benefit, it cost the Crown £850, a considerable sum of money when it was made in 1725. It still provides a (moderately) dry shod walk in the summer along the back of the Domesday settlement of Allum Green and across the Highland Water by the so called 'Roman' Bridge.

The original of this much photographed bridge is, therefore, likely to be less than three hundred years old. A little way down stream from the bridge, along the present A35, is a lone cottage now called New Forest Gatehouse but previously known as Brinton Toll Bar.

The 'Roman' Bridge on the Cut Walk which runs from the top of Emery Down Hill to Burley. Beyond the bridge the Cut Walk is now incorporated into the A35 and the road to Burley via Vinney Ridge. The bridge can also be reached from the approach road to the reptiliary

The name is probably a corruption of the nearby Brinken Wood. This was the nearest toll gate west of Lyndhurst, as closer sites are thought to have been objected to by local dignitaries such as Henry Compton who was Lord of the Manor of Minstead.

Conclusion

This book can really only offer an introduction to Lyndhurst. For those who wish to know more of its past there are numerous records and accounts to be explored.

The village has developed in a certain way - various alternatives were proposed by landowners in order to exploit its potential. One of the most intriguing was a scheme that the Commissioners of Woods worked up nearly a century ago to create a housing estate of fifty five homes and a village green on the fields surrounding Holmfield.

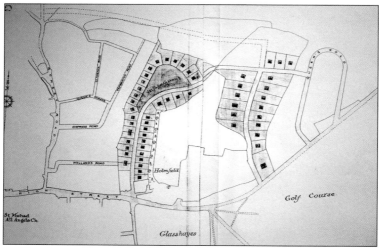

Plan for a proposed development of Lyndhurst by the Commissioners of Woods around 1910. Most of this remains as fields and recreation areas
Courtesy PRO F10/349

Most, probably, will be pleased that such schemes came to nothing and that Lyndhurst, despite mounting seasonal pressures, largely retains its village atmosphere. The New Forest is not just a summer attraction. Nothing could be more enticing than the ancient woods and heaths in autumn or spring, and in the winter, covered in frost or snow, they are spectacular. Lyndhurst, the centre of the Forest, extends a warm welcome - whatever the season.

Odd Corners Around Lyndhurst

Sources & Bibliography

Books

Babey, Georgina (com). *Images of England: New Forest*, Tempus, 2001

Clark, Anne. *The Real Alice*, Michael Joseph, 1981

Cornish, C J. *The New Forest*, Seeley & Co, 1894

De Crespigny, R C & Hutchinson, H. *The New Forest*, John Murray, 1899

Genealogical sources - Debrett's, Burke's, Walford, DNB

Gordon, Colin. *Beyond the Looking Glass*, Hodder & Stoughton, 1982

Hampshire Directories, various, 1830-1939

Hampshire Record Series - vol 3, *New Forest Documents, AD1244 - 1334*, Ed. Stagg, D J. Hampshire County Council, 1979

 - vol.12, *The Religious Census of Hampshire, 1851*, Ed.Vickers, J A. 1993

 - vol.13, *Parson and Parish in Eighteenth-Century Hampshire*, Ed. Ward, W R. 1995

Hampshire Repository, 1798-1801

Heath, F G. *Autumnal Leaves*, Sampson, Low & Co, 1881

Hudson, W H. *Hampshire Days*, Longman Green, 1903

Kenchington, F E. *The Commoners' New Forest*, Hutchinson, 1944

Lascelles, Gerald. *Thirty-Five Years in the New Forest*, E Arnold, 1915

Maxwell, W B. *Time Gathered*, Appleton-Century, New York, 1938

Munby, Julian. *Domesday Book, Hampshire* Phillimore, 1982

Pevsner/Lloyd. *The Buildings of England: Hants & I o W*, Penguin, 1973

Phillips, C J. *The New Forest Handbook*, 1876, 3rd ed 1880

Roberts, P. *Minstead: Life in a 17th Century New Forest Community,* Nova Foresta Books, 2002

Rogers, W H. *Guide to the New Forest*, editions, ca. 1895-1912

Squibb G D. [Ed], *The Visitation of Hampshire and IoW 1686,* The Harleian Society, 1991

Stagg, D J. *Snake Catchers of the New Forest*, N F Association, 1983

Steven's directory of Lymington....Lyndhurst, 1891

Tubbs, Colin R. *The New Forest*, New Forest Ninth Centenary Trust, 2001

Tweedie, G. *Hampshire's Glorious Wilderness*, Homeland Assoc. 1925

Victoria County History - Hampshire, vols. 1 & 4, 1900, 1911

Ward, Lock and Bowden's *Guide to Bournemouth, the New Forest and Winchester*, 1896/7

Wise, J R. *The New Forest: its History and Scenery*, Smith & Elder, 1863

Wood, Joanna. *Lyndhurst: The Capital of the New Forest*, Paul Cave, 1984

Periodicals and booklets

Babey, G & Roberts, P. 'Lyndhurst', *New Forest - Country Magazine*, Winter 1999

Babey, G. 'John Wise', *New Forest - Country Magazine*, Spring 2000

Babey, G. 'Women Writers', *New Forest - Country Magazine*, Summer 2002

Hampshire Advertiser, Aug 13, 1921 & Aug 12, 1922

Hampshire Independent, July 1, 1871

Hampshire Magazine, Paul Cave, October 1989

Jackman, Roy. *Lyndhurst Past and Present*, Books 1 - 5, 1969 - 1976

Jackman, Roy. *Lyndhurst Life* - several titles, Lyndhurst Historical Society, undated

Look at Lyndhurst Parish Church, Bessacarr Prints, 1994

Lyndhurst, Hampshire. Official Guide, nd, LPC. Text by R Jackman

Nova Foresta Magazine, Vol 3 No 1, Spring 1997, Vol 4 No 2, Summer 1998, Vol 6 No 3, Autumn 2000, Vol 7 No 1, Spring 2001

Queen's House, Lyndhurst. Forestry Commission booklet, undated.

Stagg D J./Roberts, P. *Verderers of the New Forest: A Brief History*, Verderers, 1997

Other Sources

Bowden-Smith, Mrs. Unpublished Mss, 1900-1

Dickenson, David. *History of Elcombes at Lyndhurst*, unpublished

Hampshire Record Office (HRO) 25M84, Lyndhurst Parish Records

HRO 149M89/R5/6457A, Bedford Accounts 1746-1771

New Forest Acts, 1698-1970

New Forest Reports, 1848, 1868, 1875, 1947

Ordnance Survey maps, 6 inch, 25 inch, various editions

Public Record Office (PRO) F10/292 High Coxlease

PRO F10/56 Lyndhurst Pony Fair 1922-40

PRO F10/349 Development proposals 1907-12

PRO S.P. Dom., Jas. I. Vol. 8, No. 76; Lyndhurst, 1604, Survey of the Manor.

Reeves, James and John. Notebook memories of the early 19th century

Richardson, King and Drivers Map of the New Forest 1789

5th Report of the Commissioners of Woods, 1789